BY ALLAN MOREY

THE DENVER
BRONCOS
STORY

TORQUE

BELLWETHER MEDIA · MINNEAPOLIS, MN

™

Are you ready to take it to the extreme? Torque books thrust you into the action-packed world of sports, vehicles, mystery, and adventure. These books may include dirt, smoke, fire, and chilling tales. **WARNING**: read at your own risk.

This edition first published in 2017 by Bellwether Media, Inc.

No part of this publication may be reproduced in whole or in part without written permission of the publisher. For information regarding permission, write to Bellwether Media, Inc., Attention: Permissions Department, 5357 Penn Avenue South, Minneapolis, MN 55419.

Library of Congress Cataloging-in-Publication Data

Names: Morey, Allan.
Title: The Denver Broncos Story / by Allan Morey.
Description: Minneapolis, MN : Bellwether Media, Inc., 2017. | Series:
   Torque: NFL Teams | Includes bibliographical references and index.
Identifiers: LCCN 2015050794 | ISBN 9781626173644 (hardcover : alk. paper)
Subjects: LCSH: Denver Broncos (Football team)–History–Juvenile literature.
Classification: LCC GV956.D37 M64 2017 | DDC 796.332/640978883–dc23
LC record available at http://lccn.loc.gov/2015050794

Printed in the United States of America, North Mankato, MN.

TABLE OF CONTENTS

In **Super Bowl** 50, the Denver Broncos go up against the Carolina Panthers. Each team has a star **quarterback**. But the **defenses** command the game.

Von Miller

In the first quarter, Denver **linebacker** Von Miller causes a **fumble**. He strips the ball from Carolina quarterback Cam Newton. The Broncos recover the ball for a touchdown!

The Panthers score a touchdown in the second quarter. Then the Broncos hold them to just a field goal in the fourth.

With minutes left, Newton is **sacked** for the sixth time. Denver goes on to win its third Super Bowl!

SCORING TERMS

END ZONE

the area at each end of a football field; a team scores by entering the opponent's end zone with the football.

EXTRA POINT

a score that occurs when a kicker kicks the ball between the opponent's goal posts after a touchdown is scored; 1 point.

FIELD GOAL

a score that occurs when a kicker kicks the ball between the opponent's goal posts; 3 points.

SAFETY

a score that occurs when a player on offense is tackled behind his own goal line; 2 points for defense.

TOUCHDOWN

a score that occurs when a team crosses into its opponent's end zone with the football; 6 points.

TWO-POINT CONVERSION

a score that occurs when a team crosses into its opponent's end zone with the football after scoring a touchdown; 2 points.

The Broncos are a Colorado team with a special home-field advantage. They play in Denver, the "Mile High City." There, they are used to the thin mountain air.

Opponents can struggle at
1 mile (1.6 kilometers) above
sea level. They are often
left breathless trying to defeat
the Orange and Blue.

The Broncos play home games at Sports Authority Field at Mile High. It is often just called Mile High.

The stadium has been sold out for every game since it opened in 2001. But Denver's sellout streak goes back even further. It began in 1970 at the old stadium!

SPORTS AUTHORITY FIELD AT MILE HIGH

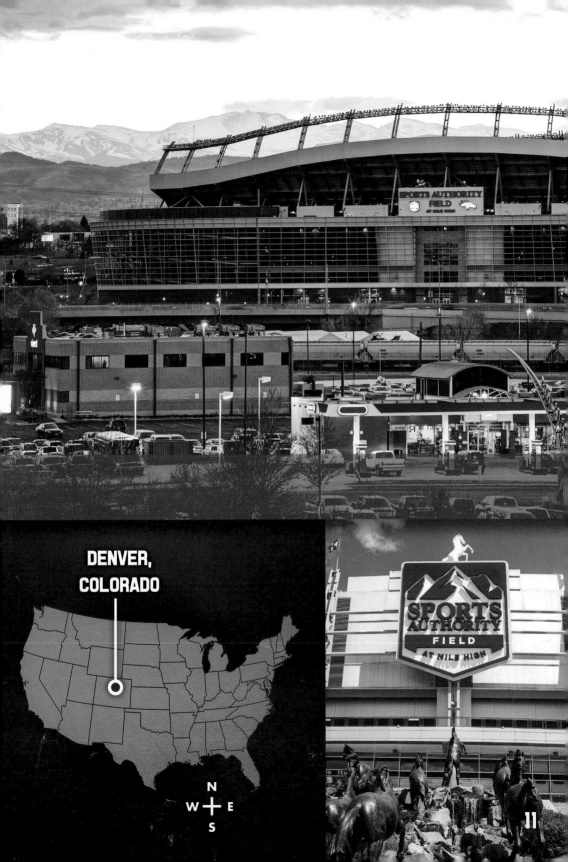

DENVER, COLORADO

The Broncos joined the National Football League (NFL) in 1970. They play in the American Football **Conference** (AFC). They are part of the West **Division**.

The West Division includes the Kansas City Chiefs, San Diego Chargers, and Oakland Raiders. The Raiders are one of Denver's biggest **rivals**.

NFL DIVISIONS

AFC

AFC NORTH

BALTIMORE **RAVENS**

CINCINNATI **BENGALS**

CLEVELAND **BROWNS**

PITTSBURGH **STEELERS**

AFC EAST

BUFFALO **BILLS**

MIAMI **DOLPHINS**

NEW ENGLAND **PATRIOTS**

NEW YORK **JETS**

AFC SOUTH

HOUSTON **TEXANS**

INDIANAPOLIS **COLTS**

JACKSONVILLE **JAGUARS**

TENNESSEE **TITANS**

AFC WEST

DENVER **BRONCOS**

KANSAS CITY **CHIEFS**

OAKLAND **RAIDERS**

SAN DIEGO **CHARGERS**

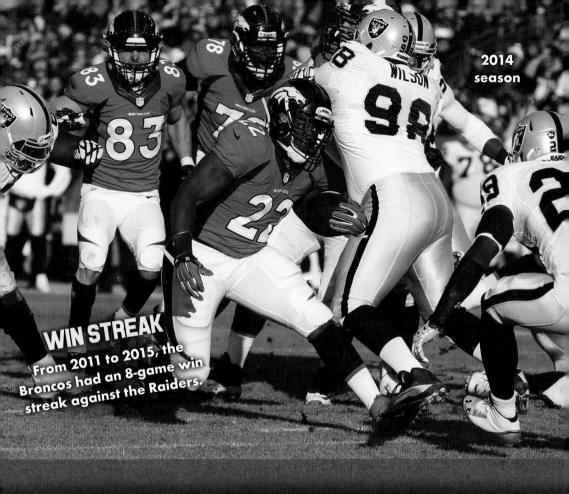

2014 season

WIN STREAK

From 2011 to 2015, the Broncos had an 8-game win streak against the Raiders.

 NFC

NFC **NORTH**

 CHICAGO
BEARS

 DETROIT
LIONS

 GREEN BAY
PACKERS

 MINNESOTA
VIKINGS

NFC **EAST**

 DALLAS
COWBOYS

 NEW YORK
GIANTS

 PHILADELPHIA
EAGLES

 WASHINGTON
REDSKINS

NFC **SOUTH**

 ATLANTA
FALCONS

 CAROLINA
PANTHERS

NEW ORLEANS
SAINTS

 TAMPA BAY
BUCCANEERS

NFC **WEST**

 ARIZONA
CARDINALS

LOS ANGELES
RAMS

 SAN FRANCISCO
49ERS

 SEATTLE
SEAHAWKS

The Broncos formed in 1959. They played in the American Football League (AFL) from 1960 to 1969. Then the AFL joined the NFL in 1970.

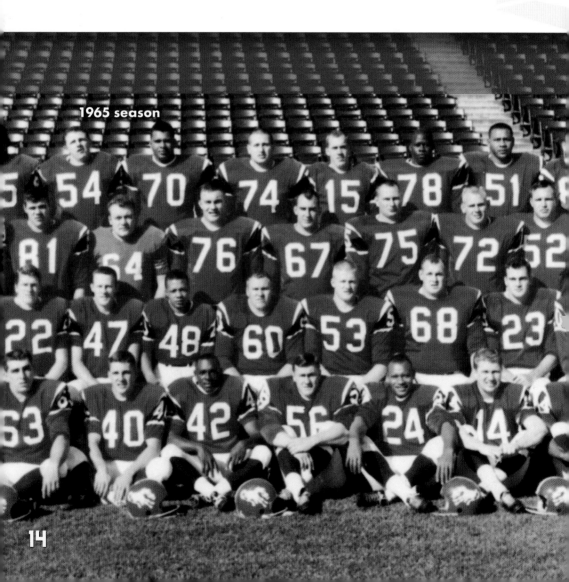

1965 season

Success first came in 1977. The Broncos ended the season with a 12 – 2 record. Then **playoff** wins brought them to their first Super Bowl.

John
Elway

In 1983, the Broncos traded for **rookie** quarterback John Elway. He led the team to five Super Bowls, including two wins.

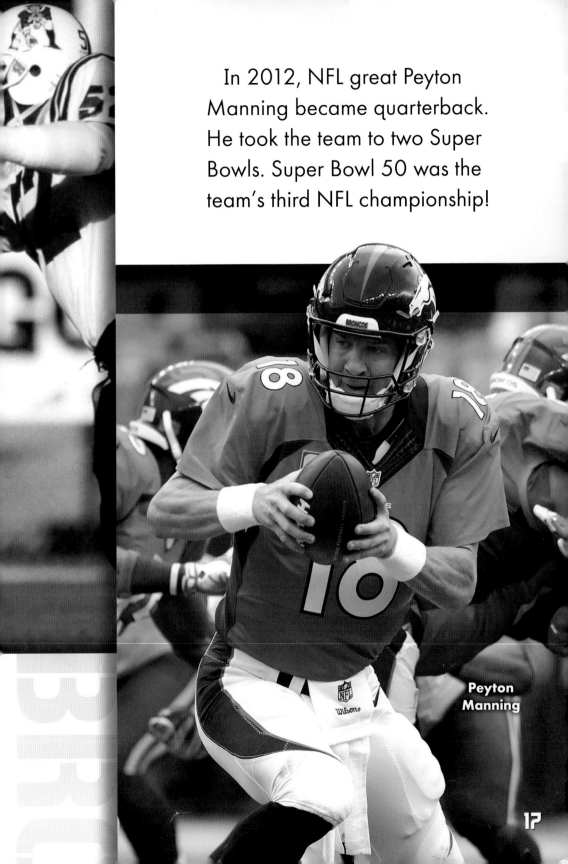

In 2012, NFL great Peyton Manning became quarterback. He took the team to two Super Bowls. Super Bowl 50 was the team's third NFL championship!

Peyton Manning

BRONCOS
TIMELINE

1998

Won Super Bowl 32, beating the Green Bay Packers

31 FINAL SCORE **24**

1960

Joined the AFL

1970

Joined the NFL

1978

Made their first Super Bowl appearance, but lost to the Dallas Cowboys

10 FINAL SCORE **27**

1983

Traded for Hall-of-Fame quarterback John Elway

1999

Won Super Bowl 33, beating the Atlanta Falcons

34   FINAL SCORE   **19**

2016

Won Super Bowl 50, beating the Carolina Panthers

24   FINAL SCORE   **10**

2013

Set an NFL scoring record with 606 points in a season

2001

First played at Sports Authority Field at Mile High

2011

Drafted linebacker Von Miller

The Broncos are famous for their 1977 defense. It was called the "Orange Crush." Linebacker Randy Gradishar led the charge.

Randy Gradishar

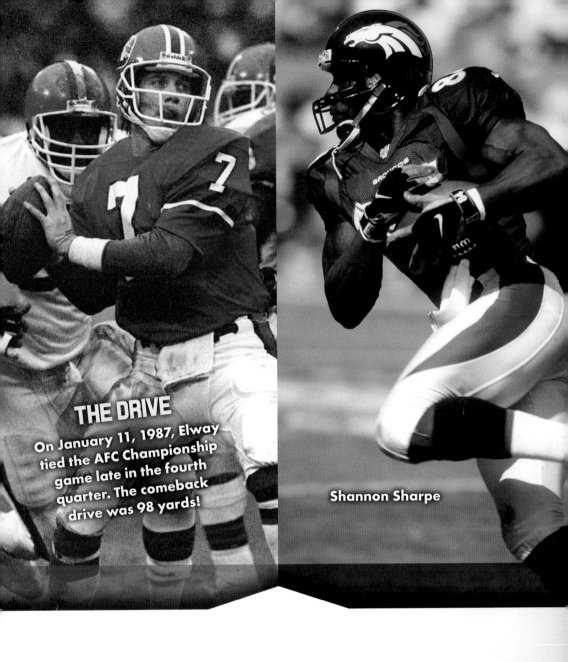

THE DRIVE

On January 11, 1987, Elway tied the AFC Championship game late in the fourth quarter. The comeback drive was 98 yards!

Shannon Sharpe

Elway was the team's leader on **offense** in the 1980s and 1990s. He had a talent for fourth-quarter comebacks. **Tight end** Shannon Sharpe helped with many last-minute plays.

Running back Terrell Davis **rushed** for the Broncos in Super Bowl 32. He scored three touchdowns. This earned him the Most Valuable Player (MVP) award for the game.

Von Miller won the MVP award for Super Bowl 50. The star linebacker forced fumbles and racked up 2.5 quarterback sacks.

BRONCOS

TEAM GREATS

RANDY GRADISHAR
LINEBACKER
1974-1983

JOHN ELWAY
QUARTERBACK
1983-1998

STEVE ATWATER
SAFETY
1989-1998

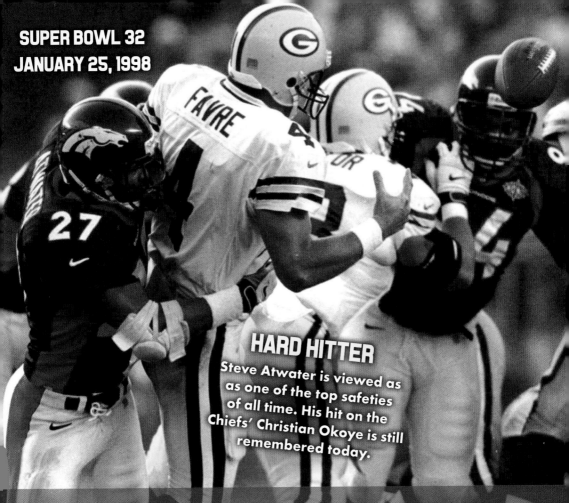

HARD HITTER

Steve Atwater is viewed as as one of the top safeties of all time. His hit on the Chiefs' Christian Okoye is still remembered today.

SHANNON SHARPE
TIGHT END
1990-1999, 2002-2003

TERRELL DAVIS
RUNNING BACK
1995-2001

VON MILLER
LINEBACKER
2011-PRESENT

The Broncos have enthusiastic fans. Home games begin with loud cheers for Thunder. This horse is a team mascot. He leads the Broncos onto the field.

THUNDER I, II, AND III
Three Arabian horses have been called Thunder. Thunder Sr. was the first in 1993.

At each sold-out home game, the announcer calls out the number of ticket holders who did not show up to Mile High. Fans boo the no-shows.

Denver fans do more than just yell.
They stomp their feet, too. This is to make
"Rocky Mountain Thunder."

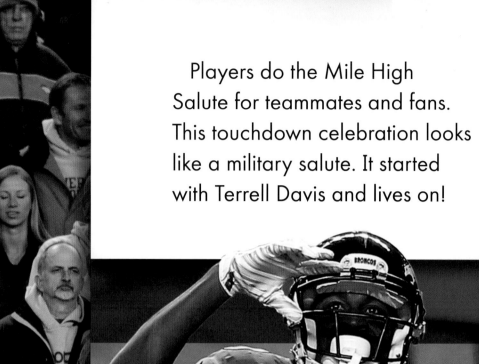

Players do the Mile High Salute for teammates and fans. This touchdown celebration looks like a military salute. It started with Terrell Davis and lives on!

Mile High Salute

MORE ABOUT THE
BRONCOS

Team name:
Denver Broncos

Team name explained:
Named after broncos,
wild or half-tamed horses

**Nicknames: Orange Crush,
Orange and Blue**

**Joined NFL: 1970
(AFL from 1960-1969)**

Conference: **AFC**

Division: **West**

Main rivals: **Kansas City Chiefs,
Oakland Raiders**

Hometown:
Denver, Colorado

Training camp location: UCHealth
Training Center, Englewood, Colorado

DENVER

COLORADO

Home stadium name:
Sports Authority Field at Mile High

Stadium opened: 2001

Seats in stadium: 76,125

Logo: A horse's head
with an orange mane

Colors: Orange,
navy blue, white

Mascots: Thunder and Miles

GLOSSARY

conference—a large grouping of sports teams that often play one another

defenses—groups of players who try to stop opposing teams from scoring

division—a small grouping of sports teams that often play one another; usually there are several divisions of teams in a conference.

fumble—a loose ball that is still in play

linebacker—a player on defense whose main job is to make tackles and stop passes; a linebacker stands just behind the defensive linemen.

offense—the group of players who try to move down the field and score

playoff—a game played after the regular NFL season is over; playoff games determine which teams play in the Super Bowl.

quarterback—a player on offense whose main job is to throw and hand off the ball

rivals—teams that are long-standing opponents

rookie—a first-year player in a sports league

running back—a player on offense whose main job is to run with the ball

rushed—ran with the ball

sacked—tackled for a loss of yards; players on defense can sack quarterbacks.

sea level—the height of the sea's surface

Super Bowl—the championship game for the NFL

tight end—a player on offense whose main jobs are to catch passes and block for teammates

TO LEARN MORE

AT THE LIBRARY

Burgess, Zack. *Meet the Denver Broncos.* Chicago, Ill.: Norwood House Press, 2016.

Howell, Brian. *Denver Broncos.* Mankato, Minn.: Child's World, 2015.

Scheff, Matt. *Superstars of the Denver Broncos.* Mankato, Minn.: Amicus, 2014.

ON THE WEB

Learning more about the Denver Broncos is as easy as 1, 2, 3.

1. Go to www.factsurfer.com.

2. Enter "Denver Broncos" into the search box.

3. Click the "Surf" button and you will see a list of related web sites.

With factsurfer.com, finding more information is just a click away.

INDEX